DO NOT DISTURB!

The Deutsche Nationalbibliothek lists this publication in the
Deutsche Nationalbibliografie; detailed bibliographic data are
available in the Internet at http://dnb.dnb.de

ISBN 978-3-03768-200-5
© 2016 by Braun Publishing AG
www.braun-publishing.ch

1st edition 2016

Editor: Manuela Roth
Text editing and translation: Judith Vonberg
Art direction: Michaela Prinz, Berlin
Reproduction: Bild1Druck GmbH, Berlin

MANUELA ROTH

DO NOT DISTURB!
HEAVENLY HONEYMOON RETREATS

BRAUN

CONTENT

PREFACE

Congratulations! You've found the one, your soul mate, the person you want by your side in the next part of your life, the person you want to share everything with! After the spectacular wedding celebration usually comes the honeymoon. A time to relax and begin your shared, happy future together. A trip to foster togetherness, to concern yourself only with each other. A time to indulge and take pleasure, to switch off and refuel.

But where should you go? Walk hand in hand along a glistening white beach and enjoy a sunset together? Or see elephants and lions on safari in the African grasslands? Or hike through the mountains of Canada, go fishing and barbecue your catch on a campfire? Or maybe immerse yourselves in the pulsating cultural life of a metropolis? Whatever you decide, everything must be perfect on the honeymoon. An exclusive room

or bungalow and exceptional service are top of the list. Even better if it comes with a personal butler, privy to your every whim. This need not remain a dream; it can become reality! In this book you will find a selection of hotels that leave no wish unfulfilled and offer a unique and unforgettable holiday experience. Each excels in something special, whether the location, the service, the activities offered or the culinary delicacies. Food can also be a way to the heart of your loved one! All in all, the perfect beginning to this new chapter of your lives.

Visit the hotel "Post Ranch Inn" on the Big Sur coastal strip on America's West Coast, and enjoy breathtaking nature. The hotel's organically formed structure and natural materials accentuate the beauty of the coastal landscape. Here you can contemplate the ocean or gaze at the star-filled night sky from your private residence. Or would you rather immerse yourself in the turbulence of New York City? In "The Ludlow", one hotel presented here, all of Manhattan lays itself at the feet of newlyweds in the Skybox Loft – just make sure you've got a good head for heights! Drink in a 180-degree view of the hustle and bustle below. Find relaxation beneath the Caribbean sun at the remarkable "Jade Mountain". Its sanctuaries boast private infinity pools and are completely open to the outside, the fourth wall entirely absent. Guests themselves become part of their surroundings and look on while nature unfolds before them, as if upon a theater stage. The "St James Paris", the only chateau hotel in the city of love, throws open its gates and invites you to relax in its fairytale interiors after a day spent exploring the city. Boasting a history rich with tradition, the "Hotel Londra Palace", near the Piazza San Marco in the heart of Venice, invites you to explore the watery city and to enjoy the Italian dolce vita. Those who prefer a little more adventure ought to go on an

African safari! Guests at "Abu Camp" in Botswana can live amongst a real elephant herd. Nowhere else in Africa is it possible to sleep with elephants beneath the stars. A unique chance to submerge in the sensuous world of Africa and create an unforgettable memory! "North Island" in the Seychelles offers a different but equally unique experience of nature. The small island has been lovingly recultivated, newly colonized with indigenous trees and animal species that had previously disappeared. A small luxury hotel supports the team in their task. It comprises eleven individual villas, each made of environmentally friendly materials. Despite the simplicity, nothing is lacking – a private chef will even prepare regional delicacies in the comfort of your own villa. In India's Ranthambore National Park the "Aman-i-Khás" welcomes its guests in ten expansive and luxuriously furnished tents. From here, you can take a guided tour to see tigers, leopards and crocodiles. Enjoy the perfect end to a thrilling day with dinner on your private deck or around a communal campfire.

Whether you're recently engaged and seeking inspiration for your honeymoon, or want to celebrate your anniversary or jubilee in intimate togetherness, you will be seized with wanderlust as you browse these pages! Board the train of love and be swept away to the world's most beautiful locations and most remarkable hotels. At every hotel and retreat presented here, guests can expect a truly exceptional experience, the perfect way to celebrate you and your exceptional union. Pack your bags and take a plane together to seventh heaven!

Clayoquot Wilderness Resort offers remote Canadian wilderness vacations, but behind the five-star cuisine, the spa and the great white tents with their fluffy duvets and antiques, there is a deep and meaningful commitment to restoring the land. With only 20 luxury guest tents the Resort offers an exclusive and personal environment for all of its visitors. Simplicity, elegance and comfort combine in the design of the tents. Wooden furnishings, comfortable sofas and beautiful fabrics create a homely but sophisticated atmosphere. Active newlyweds will love the personalized daily wilderness activities, from surfing or hiking to kayaking and horse riding. Wildlife viewing is also part of daily life, whether guests go in search of black bears and whales or see the wildlife on the outskirts of camp, kept there by a team of well-trained dogs. An outdoor lounge and gaming tents provide plentiful entertainment for less adventurous guests.

CLAYOQUOT WILDERNESS RESORT
TOFINO (BC), CANADA

Architect/designer: Bill Clark
No. of tents: 20
Recommended tent: Deluxe Outpost Tent
Type of cuisine offered: Canadian regional
Activities: surfing, hiking, kayaking, riding, archery, mountain biking, rock climbing, spa

Explore, where few have gone before...
Rustic seclusion and indulgent,
luxurious comfort.

Recline in splendor in the Deluxe Outpost Tent, a vast haven of billowing white canvas. Escape from the world into an exclusive interior, its opulent rugs, oil lamps, antique dresses and abundant candles soothing the soul and enchanting the senses.

Opened in the summer of 2008, Cavallo Point Lodge is an enchanting and environmentally sustainable "base camp" where the city's urban edge meets the rugged Marin coast. Once the site of the Fort Baker military base, today meticulously restored turn-of-the-century officer's quarters and sensitively designed new buildings respect the site's stalwart history and majestic natural setting. The 74 newly constructed contemporary rooms and suites, set on a hillside, offer spectacular views of the Golden Gate Bridge through floor-to-ceiling windows. Cavallo Point Lodge's new rooms feature sustainable design and construction with solar power, radiant heat floors, renewable materials, organic bedding and linens, and natural amenities appropriate to the lodge's national park setting. Newlyweds will love the lodge's upscale amenities and Healing Arts Center & Spa with 11 treatment rooms integrating the best cultural healing practices from around the world. A heated outdoor meditation pool is a focal point for guests, as well as the Tea Bar, featuring teas, snacks and herbal tonics.

CAVALLO POINT LODGE
SAN FRANCISCO (CA), USA

Architect/designer: Leddy Maytum Stacy Architects
No. of rooms/villas: 68 historic rooms and suites, 74 newly constructed contemporary rooms and suites
Recommended room: Contemporary Deluxe King
Type of cuisine offered: French-inspired, ingredient-driven Northern California cuisine
Activities: spa, cooking school, yoga, walking tours, hiking, biking, bird watching and kayaking

13

The Contemporary Deluxe King suite features bamboo furnishings, a gas fireplace, a window seat and a patio or deck with outdoor furnishings and all manner of luxury amenities.

Enjoy romantic seclusion in an inviting suite and San Francisco excitement just across the Golden Gate Bridge. There's so much to share – breathtaking views from your hotel room, soothing spa treatments for couples, award-winning dining, a hike to see the sunset ...

High atop the cliffs of Big Sur, 365 meter above the Pacific Ocean, sits Post Ranch Inn, a sanctuary for the soul. With natural architecture embracing the coast's dramatic beauty, the 41 rooms blend rustic elegance, comfort and privacy with panoramic ocean or mountain views. The coast-side rooms seem to soar, cantilevered off the mountain, while the mountain-side houses curve around old-growth trees. Some are built on nine-foot stilts to protect the delicate root balls below. The structures' materials – reclaimed wood, glass, steel and stone – further enhance the sense of harmony with nature. Ideal for romance, relaxation and rejuvenation, this resort is the ultimate destination for newlyweds seeking luxurious escape. The Wine Spectator Grand-Award winning Sierra Mar restaurant offers exquisite dining with a menu that changes daily, complimentary gourmet breakfast buffet and a spectacular setting with endless ocean views. Guests can relax by the pools, rejuvenate with an in-room massage or spa treatment, or explore all that nature has to offer.

POST RANCH INN
BIG SUR (CA), USA

Architect: Mickey Muennig
No. of rooms/villas: 41 rooms, suites and private homes
Recommended room: Coast House
Type of cuisine offered: fresh, locally sourced ingredients along with bold, primal flavors
Activities: spa, yoga, hiking, nightly star gazing

Inspired by the surrounding redwood trees, the circular Coast House boasts a private entrance, soft leather couch and cozy fireplace.

High atop the cliffs of Big Sur sits a sanctuary for the soul. Offering a unique ocean view, it is the ultimate destination for romance, relaxation and rejuvenation.

19

Designed by Robert T. Lyons and built by the famous developer brothers Bing and Bing, Gramercy Park Hotel opened its doors in 1925 and was soon at the center of New York's haute bohème. The recent redesign by John Pawson and Julian Schnabel, incorporating unique furnishings, paintings and sculptures, establishes the hotel as a living work of art. The creative flair of the public areas is continued in the 185 rooms and suites. Each of the generously sized rooms offers a unique composition of colors, materials, art and objects, with leather chairs, and imported, hand-knotted rugs.

Deep red velvet curtains with customized bronze rails frame mahogany windows and complete the opulent ambience. Honeymooners will particularly enjoy the stunning roof garden with terrace and the hotel's two bars – spaces where people can immerse themselves in the real, authentic New York. With guests from all walks of life including New York and international societies, Gramercy Park Hotel is a hotel that truly captures Manhattan.

GRAMERCY PARK HOTEL
NEW YORK (NY), USA

Architect: Robert T. Lyons, John Pawson
Interior designer: Julian Schnabel
No. of rooms: 185 rooms and suites
Recommended room: Park View Suite
Type of cuisine offered: Italian/Roman
Activities: spa, fitness, sightseeing, cultural activities

Fabulous views of historical Gramercy Park, a luxurious king-size bed topped with imported Italian linens and an elegant living room are just a few of the features to be enjoyed in the Park View Suite.

Humphrey Bogart was married here,
Bob Marley was a regular guest and John F.
Kennedy played in Gramercy Park when his
family spent several months at the hotel.

Trendsetting hoteliers Sean MacPherson, Ira Drukier and Richard Born made their Lower East Side debut with The Ludlow, modeling guestrooms after chic Manhattan loft and studio apartments that capture the vivid history and urban charm of the iconic neighborhood. The hotel features 184 guestrooms, including 20 suites, all with breath-taking vistas of New York City's landmarks and bridges. Each combines simplicity with elegant design. The property includes the Lobby Lounge, which features a rotating art display curated by Vito Schnabel, an all-season outdoor "secret" gar- den, a lobby bar with signature cocktail menu by Major Food Group's Thomas Waugh and light bites, and the ground-floor restaurant, Dirty French, helmed by Mario Carbone, Rich Torrisi and Jeff Zalaznick. Perfect for newlyweds looking for a taste of big city life, this hotel offers stylish design and cosmopolitan sophistication married with old-world charm and home-style comfort.

THE LUDLOW
NEW YORK (NY), USA

Architect/designer: Sean MacPherson
No. of rooms: 184 rooms including 20 suites
Recommended room: Skybox Loft
Type of cuisine offered: French classics with a
New York sensibility
Activities: sightseeing, cultural activities

Grab cocktails and light bites at the Lobby Bar, walk over the Williamsburg Bridge, and check out legendary Russ & Daughters, knish haven Yonah Schimmel, Katz's Deli, or Ludlow Guitars, all just steps away.

The zenith of sophistication, the Skybox Loft is the supreme honeymoon destination. Boasting Bellino Fine Linens and Red Flower bath products, the loft offers 180-degree views of Manhattan.

27

The Tides South Beach is located in the Art Deco district in Miami's South Beach area. Known as "The Diva of Ocean Drive", the hotel's design was richly influenced by the Art Deco movement. The simple façade rises high into the sky, while neutral tones and natural wood dominate the interiors. The resort comprises 35 studio suites (averaging 51 square meter in size, amongst the largest rooms on South Beach), seven junior suites, and three exclusive penthouse suites (ranging from 83 to 205 square meter in size), all with ocean views and state-of-the-art amenities. The restaurant's international cuisine can be enjoyed either in the exquisite lobby or outdoors on a spacious terrace. Ideally located for the world-famous Miami Beach nightlife, honeymooners will not be short of entertainment. Yet The Tides South Beach is also a tranquil retreat from the noise and bustle, a haven of modest style and sophistication.

THE TIDES SOUTH BEACH

MIAMI BEACH (FL), USA

Architects/designers: L. Murray Dixon, Kelly Wearstler
No. of rooms: 45 rooms and suites
Recommended room: Amber Studio Penthouse Suite
Type of cuisine offered: international
Activities: dining, shopping, nightclubs, water activities,
museums, golf, tennis

Perfect for honeymoons, the Amber Suite is the epitome of luxury. This intimate studio penthouse suite boasts every desirable amenity, from king-size bed to spa-style bathroom and private outdoor terrace.

The "Diva of Ocean Drive" is the perfect location to enjoy all South Beach has to offer.

The Viceroy Riviera Maya is a serene hideaway that merges luxury amenities with a lush jungle ambiance dense with ferns, palms and guava trees. Set on a white sand beach and lapped by the turquoise waters of the Caribbean, this resort is a sublime destination for newlyweds. The spacious and elegantly appointed villas feature a private patio and plunge pool, outdoor shower, and a high-ceiling thatched-palapa roof that resonates with the jungle environment. Guest amenities include a lagoon pool, a fine-dining restaurant and seaside grill, day beds at the beach, a fitness center and a library lounge. The resort also has its own pier where honeymooners can enjoy sunbathing, massages and romantic dinners. Special services for couples offered include the "Plunge Pool Romantic Turndown" and the "Aphrodisiac Shower Experience". Both set the scene for a sensual evening in an evocative private ambiance under the stars. Nestled in a lush tropical landscape, the resort's spa offers a range of treatments inspired by the healing techniques of the ancient Mayans, whose holistic philosophy also inspired the spa's circular structure.

VICEROY RIVIERA MAYA
PLAYA DEL CARMEN, MEXICO

Architect: GVA & Associates
Interior designer: Arquitectura de Interiores
No. of villas: 41 private villas
Recommended villa: Ocean View Two Level Villa
Type of cuisine offered: refined Mexican cuisine in La Marea, Mediterranean-Mexican menu cooked on wood-burning grills in Coral Grill
Activities: swimming in the Caribbean Sea, fitness center, golf, horseback riding, polo, fishing, parasailing, kite surfing, skydiving, bird watching, nature walks, tennis, jungle tours, artisanal cocktail mixology class, master grilling class

Spend your days drifting away on the oceanside palapas and enjoy an afternoon picnic of savory bites and tropical cocktails.

Enjoy a romantic evening for two by the plunge pool, complete with lit votive candles and flower petals. Or take a stroll onto the beach for a cooling dip in the Caribbean ocean. Whatever your desire, Ocean View Villa is the ideal destination.

Originally built as the private home of an Italian duchess, Hotel Esencia is a place where the traditions of the past come together with a cosmopolitan sense of how to live well today. Recently reimagined by a new owner with a bold and innovative outlook, this aristocratic oasis sits where the Yucatán jungle dissolves into the pristine sands of Xpu-Ha, one of the only remaining undeveloped shores of the Mayan Riviera. Hotel Esencia is now a sought-after destination for honeymooners seduced by the serene comforts of the timeless mansion. Sited on a majestic 200,000-square meter estate, the hotel comprises the Main House and 29 suites and villas where guests enjoy privacy and superb hospitality. The architecture combines clean lines and simple geometries with warm terracotta tones and serene white façades and interiors. Elegant dark wooden shutters harmonize with the rich wooden furnishings. Ideally situated far from huge resorts and the roar of pleasure boats, the immaculate bay of Xpu-Ha is a natural haven where each year sea turtles make their nests.

HOTEL ESENCIA
XPU-HA, MEXICO

Architect (original): Alfonso Nunez
Interior designers: Kevin Wendle, CS Valentin
No. of rooms/villas: 29 suites and villas
Recommended room: master suite
Type of cuisine offered: Mexico's eclectic range of regional cuisines fused with Mediterranean cooking
Activities: spa, swimming, diving, excursions, nightclubbing

37

With its panoramic views of the grounds and ocean, a king-size bed and grand terraces, the master suite is the architectural diamond of Hotel Esencia.

Attention to detail is the essence of Hotel Esencia; minimalistic design complements the tropical setting.

On a pristine stretch of Mexican coastline, 16 upscale beach bungalows dot the unspoiled coast north of Puerto Escondido. Long regarded as a top ten surfing destination, the charismatic town welcomes the new rustic glamour that complements the area's laid-back beachside vibe. Hoteliers Carlos Couturier and Moises Micha collaborated with architect Federico Rivera to create a modern take on traditional palapa beach huts. Together, they have transformed 200 meters of coastline into a sophisticated private paradise with a commitment to honor local tradition and design. The 16 beach-front bungalows boast minimalist and comfortable lines, crowned by authentic palapa rooftops and tropical wood floorboards, all sourced locally. Natural light beams through louvered wooden slats with regional curio ornamenting each room. Honeymooners will fall in love with the draped canvas hammocks, slung overlooking each hut's private plunge pool, perfect for a quick cooling dip after a sleep in the sun.

HOTEL ESCONDIDO
PUERTO ESCONDIDO, MEXICO

Architects/designers: Federico Rivera Rio, Jose Juan Rivera Rio
No. of rooms: 16 bungalows
Recommended bungalow: bungalow 1 and bungalow 16
Type of cuisine offered: organic, local food
Activities: surfing and other water activities

For couples addicted to music, there is an underground club for celebrating their marriage in a special way.

Sit back and relax in your very own palapa, inspired by the colors of Mexico. Take a dip in your private pool, unwind in the chill-out zone or simply savor the spectacular views.

Located 30 minutes away from the town of San Pedro, the largest on Belize's Ambergris Caye, is El Secreto, an intimate 13-villa resort surrounded by the lush and natural beauty of an island setting. Accessible only by boat to the hotel's private pier, El Secreto is a unique experience in a region that remains largely undiscovered. Each thatched-roof villa has been designed with the locale in mind, the impressive environs taking center-stage in each accommodation by way of ocean views and landscaped grounds. Local Belizean tropical woods and regional design elements are incorporated throughout, while beamed ceilings, earth-toned textiles and rattan furniture introduce a healthy dose of laid-back Caribbean cool to El Secreto. This boutique retreat is ideal for newlyweds, offering high-end comfort and modern conveniences alongside a unique experience of the natural world. The restaurant delivers guests the best organic ingredients the island has to offer and the Ikal spa acts as the ultimate gateway to total relaxation with its program of Mayan influenced treatments.

EL SECRETO
AMBERGRIS CAYE, BELIZE

Architect/designer: Abraham Saade
No. of villas: 13 villas
Recommended villa: Sea Villa
Type of cuisine offered: international cuisine with Belizean specialties
Activities: spa, diving, fishing, snorkeling, excursions, helicopter tours

45

Boasting a full ocean view, the Sea Villa is the epitome of luxury accommodation. Highlights include the king-sized bed, hammock, outdoor shower and hot tub, walk-in closet, Jacuzzi and terrace.

For those seeking an intimate, barefoot luxury experience to celebrate their recent nuptials, El Secreto offers authentically designed villas, scenic surroundings that include the crystal blue waters of the Caribbean and a lush tropical landscape, distinctive amenities, and a variety of experiences for couples to enjoy together.

Located on St. Lucia's south-western Caribbean coastline, Jade Mountain Resort rises high above the beach front resort of Anse Chastanet. Its organic architecture pays homage to St. Lucia's stunning scenic beauty. The bold design features individual bridges leading to infinity pool sanctuaries and rugged stone-faced columns. In each sanctuary, bedroom, living area and private infinity pool blend together, forming grand platforms that seem to extent into the natural world beyond. With the fourth wall entirely absent, Jade Mountain's sanctuaries are stage-like settings from which to embrace the full glory of St. Lucia's Pitons World Heritage Site and the Caribbean Sea. Newlyweds can look forward to sampling James Beard Award winner Chef Allen Susser's "Jade Cuisine" before relaxing on the Celestial Terrace, perfect for sunset cocktails or star-gazing. The resort offers a wide range of spa services, while the restaurants, bars, boutiques and sport facilities at Anse Chastanet can be easily accessed by foot or resort shuttle.

JADE MOUNTAIN
SOUFRIÈRE, ST. LUCIA, WEST INDIES

Architect: Nick Troubetzkoy
No. of rooms: 24 infinity pool sanctuaries, 5 sky jacuzzi suites
Recommended room/villa: Sun Sanctuary
Type of cuisine offered: exotic with a history of fusion
Activities: spa, swimming, snorkeling, diving, bird watching, biking, kayaking, tennis, excursions

The very essence of Jade Mountain is the celebration of life and love. From the architecture to the spectacular setting, the stage is set for the honeymoon of a lifetime.

Each infinity pool sanctuary is a carefully designed, individual work of art and architecture where indoor and outdoor mingle in perfect union. Relax by the pool and absorb unrivalled views of the Pitons and the Caribbean Sea.

BOUCAN is a unique hotel owned by British Chocolatier Hotel Chocolat set high amongst the rainforest and sun-dappled cocoa groves of Saint Lucia's oldest plantation, Rabot Estate. Luxury and style come together in the midst of spectacular natural beauty in this exclusive resort. Newly-weds can relax and unwind, treat themselves to a soothing Cocoa Juvenate spa treatment, explore the beautiful surroundings, take a tour or walk the cocoa trails. Foodies will particularly relish the hotel's pioneering cacao cuisine menu. Created to sit perfectly in the stunning natural beauty of their rainforest surroundings, the lodges at BOUCAN are a unique blend of Saint Lucian charm and sleek contemporary style. Warm woods, rough stone and natural hues combine to create a sense of tranquility and harmony with nature. All rooms are positioned to catch the cooling breeze and are furnished with premium luxury and comfort in mind. Evenings can be spent absorbing the spectacular views or sipping a fresh Cacao Bellini in the stylish bar.

BOUCAN
SOUFRIÈRE, SAINT LUCIA, WEST INDIES

Architect/designer: Phil Buckley
No. of rooms: 14 lodges
Recommended room: Luxe Lodge
Type of cuisine offered: Cocoa cuisine
Activities: spa, swimming, excursions, boat trips

Boasting dramatic views of the Pitons and the Caribbean Sea from their private verandas, the hotel's eight Luxe Lodges are the ideal romantic destination. With a super king-size four-poster bed and open-sky twin rainforest shower, newlyweds can enjoy luxury at its finest.

Thanks to its aphrodisiac effect, chocolate was a culinary symbol for the gods of love in the Aztec culture.

Kurà Design Villas, a small eco-friendly, boutique hotel with six luxury and hillside villas, is located on the southern coast of Costa Rica, at the spot where the rainforest-covered mountains meet the coastline. Starting with a commitment to protect the local environment, founders and owners biologist Alejandra Umana and architect Martin Wells are Costa Ricans who wanted to share their love of the country's biodiversity and beauty with a hospitality experience that enhanced, yet did not compete with the surrounding wilderness. Set on an impressive mountain ridge overlooking the Pacific Ocean, Kurà was created around a minimalist design that allows the lush mountain top rainforest to blend in with the elegance of the accommodations. All villas are open-floor concept and showcase features including king-sized beds, bamboo ceilings, sliding-glass doors and spacious terraces. Stunning ocean views and a saltwater infinity pool make this a perfect destination for newlyweds.

KURA DESIGN VILLAS
UVITA DE OSA, COSTA RICA

Architect: Martin Wells
No. of villas: 6 villas
Recommended villa: Suite Villa
Type of cuisine offered: Costa Rican fusion cuisine
Activities: spa, waterfall rapelling, snorkeling, whale watching, hiking, horseback riding, kayaking, zipline, yoga, surfing

Picture yourselves in an oversized villa surrounded by nothing but lush jungle. The open façade allows breathtaking views of the ocean where the sun sets gloriously every day.

Experience the ultimate fusion of luxury, tranquility and comfort in the Suite Villa. The open-floor design, luxurious amenities and breathtaking forest and ocean views will arouse the senses and sweep you into sheer ecstasy.

59

Embraced to the north by the resplendent panorama of miles of virgin Atlantic outback and to the east by the turquoise open sea, Kenoa Resort is a paragon of luxury and tranquility. This eco-chic design resort has been created with attention paid to the smallest details, ensuring the best possible guest experience. Natural materials and neutral tones are used throughout the resort, which engages sensitively and harmoniously with its natural environment. Rustic pillars and floors of sand create the impression of esthetic unity between the manmade and natural worlds. Honeymoon-ers will particularly enjoy the privacy afforded them at this resort. Specially trained attendants provide for your every whim without ever being intrusive, allowing guests to create their own private, intimate space, an escape from the world outside. Newlyweds will love to explore the lagoon complex with its untouched mangrove and Gunga beach, one of the most beautiful beaches in Brazil.

KENOA - EXCLUSIVE BEACH SPA & RESORT

BARRA DE SÃO MIGUEL, BRAZIL

Architect: Osvaldo Tenório
No. of rooms/villas: 11 suites and 12 villas
Recommended villa: Kenoa Villa
Type of cuisine offered: fusion of international and Brazilian cuisine by César Santos
Activities: spa, oyster farm experience, sports, excursions

You will find that the soft lights, the subtle tones and the soothing sounds of Kenoa provide the seeds and fertile soil to generate memories that will last.

A rustic luxury residence in harmony with nature's seascape, Kenoa Villa is truly one-of-a-kind. Boasting a heated infinity-edged plunge pool and a traditional Japanese ofurotub made of fragrant hand-planed cedar wood, this villa offers rejuvenation to every guest.

A highlight of Berlin's Kurfürstendamm in bygone days, Hotel Zoo is once again resplendent. Designer Dayna Lee has restored and accentuated its former glories, while infusing the space with a contemporary feel. Originally built as a private residence for an affluent family, it was converted into an upscale hotel in 1911 and became host to the Berlin International Film Festival in 1951. It offers spacious rooms and suites, appointed with bespoke furnishings and imbued with a soupçon of Berlin brashness. High ceilings, luxurious materials and an eclectic array of furniture accumulated over generations combine to create an eccentric but highly sophisticated destination near Berlin's train station Zoologischer Garten. In the heart of the hotel, next to a glowing fireplace, guests can enjoy a classic cocktail or dance to the rhythms of world-famous DJs. Experience a taste of the celebrated bar and cocktail culture of 1920s Berlin, Paris and New York, right here in Hotel Zoo. Honeymooners can enjoy quieter moments in the winter garden, the ideal spot for a romantic encounter.

HOTEL ZOO BERLIN
BERLIN, GERMANY

Architect/designer: Dayna Lee
No. of rooms/suites: 131 rooms and 14 suites
Recommended room/suite: King Suite
Type of cuisine offered: modern culinary and aromatic impressions
Activities: sightseeing, cultural excursions, shopping

Savor the view of the legendary Kurfürstendamm
from the luxury of Hotel Zoo's King Suite. Relax
beneath the rain shower or in the free-standing
bath after an exhilarating day in the heart of Berlin
and enjoy every technological amenity in the midst
of elegance and pure comfort.

With thoughtful attention to detail and the preservation of original building elements, the space is infused with New York flair and London townhouse elegance.

For nearly a century, this grand neo-classical mansion hosted some of the most talented French students at the behest of the Thiers Foundation, established by Mrs Dosne-Thiers in memory of her husband, the French President Adolphe Thiers. In the heart of Paris' most fashionable neighborhood, it is now the capital's only chateau-hotel, as well as the home of the private Saint James Club. The house has been redesigned by the dream-maker Bambi Sloan who added her touch of extravagance to its homely atmosphere. The combination of opulence and tradition in the interior reflects the grand façade and surrounding gardens. Newly married couples can enjoy the close proximity of the famous Avenue Foch and the luxury boutiques of Avenue Victor Hugo, before returning for a drink in the unique library-bar and to savor the gourmet cuisine of Chef Virginie Basselot. Two spa treatment rooms are reminiscent of cozy bourdoirs, while the chandeliers and Versailles parquet make the exercise room truly one-of-a-kind.

SAINT JAMES PARIS
PARIS, FRANCE

Designer: Bambi Sloan
No. of rooms: 48 rooms and suites
Recommended room: Superior Room
Type of cuisine offered: Michelin star-awarded fresh and truly seasonal cuisine
Activities: spa, fitness, sightseeing, cultural activities, shopping

The Superior Room at the Saint James Paris is named with good reason. Its striking wall mirrors, gorgeous bedside furniture and rich hues exude luxury and resonate with history.

The house has been redesigned by the dream-maker Bambi Sloan who added her touch of extravagance.

Just a few minutes from the legendary village of St. Tropez lies a place far from the crowds and noise. La Réserve Ramatuelle overlooks one of the most beautiful bays on the Côte d'Azur, with a spectacular view over the endless sea, a vast private estate nestled in the Provence garrigue (Mediterranean scrubland). A world apart, suspended between sky and sea, this hotel and spa provides a unique tête à-tête with nature. With its spectacular, streamlined volumes, created by architect Jean-Michel Wilmotte, the building appears as a contemporary vessel delicately perched overlooking the sea. Amid the chic ambience enhanced by natural materials, the subtle palette of mineral nuances is interpreted across a kaleidoscope of ochre, white and sandy tones, offering a dazzling reflection of southern light. All rooms and suites have their own terraces, some also boasting a private aromatic garden. La Réserve Ramatuelle offers honeymooners the chance to relax and rejuvenate in a secret haven of serenity.

LA RÉSERVE
RAMATUELLE, FRANCE

Architect and interior designer: Jean-Michel Wilmotte
Architect of the villas: Rémi Tessier
No. of rooms/villas: 9 rooms, 19 suites and 12 villas
Recommended room/villa: suite
Type of cuisine offered: Michelin star-awarded modern
Provençal repertoire with fresh products
Activities: spa, swimming, excursions

The suite's tasteful white and beige color scheme, generous space, designer furniture and subtle light effects combine to create an atmosphere perfectly conducive to daydreaming.

Breathtaking views, a privileged lookout on the coast, a ribbon of land which stretches lazily towards the skyline. And the Mediterranean Sea as far as the eye can see.

Ohla Hotel is a five-star boutique hotel located in the historical center of Barcelona, surrounded by three of the city's most popular sightseeing and shopping areas: the Gothic Quarter, the Born and the Eixample. Inaugurated in February 2011, its location makes it ideal as a honeymoon destination, fusing calm serenity with the bustle of downtown Barcelona. The project has left untouched the building's historical façade from 1920 and other listed elements, including the main staircase, while giving the establishment a cutting-edge, minimalist interior design that combines various textures of black, white and oak wood. The structure is particularly notable for the sculpture on the façade by world-renowned artist Frederic Amat. Gastronomically inclined newlyweds will love sampling the various cuisines on offer, while the "Kitchen-Bar" inside the kitchen at Saüc restaurant offers a direct view of the chef at work. In short, Ohla Hotel offers charm, personality and style in the center of Barcelona.

OHLA HOTEL BARCELONA
BARCELONA, SPAIN

Architects/designers: Alonso Balaguer, Daniel Isern
No. of rooms: 74 rooms and suites
Recommended room: Dome Suite
Type of cuisine offered: tapas in La Plassohla, Michelin star-awarded Catalan cuisine in Saüc
Activities: fitness, swimming, sightseeing, cultural activities

A universe of combined experiences: the serenity of a historic building juxtaposed with the hustle and bustle of monumental Barcelona, brimming with life.

Bathed in a sea of natural Mediterranean light flowing in through its vast bay windows, the Dome Suite is the Ohla Hotel's crowning glory. Revel in the suite's high ceilings and spacious sitting room and unwind on its terrace with stunning views over Barcelona.

Castell Son Claret's purist esthetics and harmonious integration with nature invite total relaxation and rejuvenation. The retreat comprises eight listed buildings with 38 suites and rooms, each unique and boasting individual character and charm. 20 rooms are housed in the main building with 18 further accommodations spread through seven neighboring buildings, grouped around a stunning Arabic fountain. Spacious and airy, the contemporary rooms exude an atmosphere of wellbeing and tranquility. Color and vibrancy are provided by artistic works created by international and Majorcan artists. An enticing gastronomic experience awaits newlyweds in the resort's Michelin star kitchen. Head chef Fernando P. Arellano uses ingredients fresh from local markets to create unique culinary masterpieces. Castell Son Claret is an oasis of relaxation and wellness, combining mild serenity, unrivaled natural environs and unmatched indulgence to create a true experience of paradise.

CASTELL SON CLARET
ES CAPDELLÁ, MALLORCA, SPAIN

Architects/designers: Klaus-Michael and Christine Kühne
No. of rooms: 38 rooms and suites
Recommended room: Pool Suite
Type of cuisine offered: Michelin star-awarded fresh and local cuisine in Zaranda, international or typical Majorcan dishes made from local, Mediterranean ingredients in Olivera
Activities: spa, swimming, fitness, cycling, hiking, excursions

Luxuriate in a Pool Suite at Castell Son Claret. From the living and dining areas to the private pool and bedroom, rest and relaxation can be found in this tranquil space.

Originality, grace and the beauty of nature are rarities that give us inner peace and strength. Castell Son Claret is a retreat which offers pure esthetics in harmony with the ever-present nature that invites you to exhale deeply and relax completely.

Over its 150 years, this historic hotel has hosted countless artists and celebrities including Tchaikovsky, D'Annunzio and Borges, who were captivated by the Londra Palace and its dream location. This heritage is surely a great attraction for any newly married couple. The hotel is located in the heart of Venice, with Piazza San Marco just a stone's throw away, as are the vaporetti and gondolas to explore the canals. One hundred windows look out over the San Marco Basin and the Lagoon, while the views over the roofs and church towers on the opposite side are no less beautiful.

Biedermeier-style furniture, tapestries and brocades adorn the elegantly decorated rooms, each of which is unique. The pride of the Londra Palace, the restaurant Do Leoni adds a creative touch to the great classic dishes of Venetian cuisine. The chef's culinary art is enhanced by the elegance of the indoor dining room, whose décor includes artistic crystal and original paintings.

HOTEL LONDRA PALACE
VENICE, ITALY

Architect: Rocco Macnoli
No. of rooms: 53 rooms and suites
Recommended room/villa: Deluxe Room
Type of cuisine offered: traditional, classic Venetian cuisine with more elaborate dishes
Activities: sightseeing, cultural activities, shopping

One hundred windows look out over the San Marco Basin and the Lagoon. However, the views over the roofs and church towers from the other side of the building are no less beautiful.

Overlooking the San Marco Basin, the Deluxe Rooms at the Londra Palace are ideal for a romantic getaway. Elegant upholstery, antique furniture and modern comforts combine in a perfect fusion of old and new.

Villa Cora is located within a centuries-old park on the hills just outside the historical center of Florence. An aristocratic residence built at the end of the nineteenth century and reflecting the architectural styles of that period, the villa is dominated by an eclectic décor and earned its reputation hosting international guests of great importance. Re-opening in 2010 after an extensive three-year restoration, Villa Cora is once again a highlight in Florence's architectural landscape and an enviable destination for newlyweds. The hotel has 46 rooms and suites, all of which were meticulously restored with the aim of conserving the original architectural style as much as possible. The main villa hosts 30 suites and rooms, while Villino Eugenia, a small guest house overlooking the Boboli Gardens, comprises 14 accommodations, each decorated and furnished according to the bourgeois styles of the late nineteenth century with ceilings representing rare and exotic subjects. La Follie is located at the edge of the park and has just two rooms, offering perfect seclusion and solitude.

VILLA CORA
FLORENCE, ITALY

No. of rooms: 46 rooms and suites
Recommended room/villa: Deluxe Room
Type of cuisine offered: classic Italian cuisine reinterpreted with seasonal products
Activities: spa, swimming, cultural activities, shopping

With views of the park and hills surrounding the spectacular city of Florence, the Deluxe Rooms of Villa Cora are the ideal destination for cultured newlyweds seeking romance. Luxuriate in the precious fabrics and antique furniture and savor the magnificent panorama from the private balcony.

Step inside the elegant and spacious rooms and you will find a profusion of architectural treasures.

This hotel is the culmination of the restoration of the village of Castiglioncello del Trinoro, nestled in the historic heart of the Val d'Orcia region and lying dormant for the past few decades. The project is the labor of love of American Michael Cioffi, who has dedicated himself to rebuilding the semi-abandoned, medieval village in a manner that pays homage to the Tuscan region. The hotel comprises a collection of three villas, a newly-restored 12th century chapel, a fine-dining restaurant and an exciting program of artistic and cultural events. Honeymooners will find sublime comfort, spectacular vistas, an outdoor swimming pool, and effortless guest services all within a stunning and charming cadre. The use of indigenous materials and reclaimed wood were central to the meticulous and authentic reconstruction of this former pensione. Local woods, Tuscan flagstone, granite and Carrara marble give each room a distinct appearance that is authentically grounded in the spirit and humble origins of the Val d'Orcia.

MONTEVERDi HOTEL & ViLLAS
CASTiGLiONCELLO DEL TRiNORO, iTALY

Interior designer: Ilaria Miani
No. of rooms/villas: 13 rooms and 3 villas
Recommended room: Il Pozzo
Type of cuisine offered: Tuscan cuisine
Activities: spa, gym, swimming, gallery, cultural activities, excursions

Monteverdi Tuscany is a sensory experience: from food and wine to art exhibitions and concert performances, guests can savor every dimension the village has to offer.

A fusion of simplicity and antique elements, Il Pozzo is the ultimate in sophisticated design. The custom-built copper bedframe is proof that this room is anything but ordinary. The large, 18th century copper bathtub is flanked by a rainfall shower, with a view of the valley.

At Casa Angelina, delicately perched above the azure Mediterranean, timeless elegance of style and service combines with cosseting accommodation, gourmet cuisine and restorative wellness therapies. Wooden floors and playful pieces of bold contemporary art add warmth and color to the sleek clean lines of the accommodations and public areas. The white décor kept immaculate by an in-house painter juxtaposes with the sparkling cerulean sea, visible from almost everywhere through floor-to-ceiling windows that frame the sea and the sky. Furnishings are eclectic and tac-tile, while discreet hi-tech elements enhance the quality of each guest's stay, but are never intrusive. A range of amenities make Casa Angelina a wonderful resort for newlyweds, from the heated indoor and outdoor pools and comprehensive range of beauty and wellness treatments to private boat trips and the seasonal, locally sourced Mediterranean cuisine available in the gourmet restaurant.

CASA ANGELINA LiFESTYLE
PRAiANO, iTALY

Architects/designers: Francesco Savarese, Gennaro Fusco
No. of rooms: 39 rooms and suites in the main building,
4 rooms on the beach
Recommended room: Junior Suite
Type of cuisine offered: territorial Neapolitan cuisine
Activities: spa, swimming, boat tours, water sports, sightseeing,
trekking, shopping

From every angle, indulge in the panoramic vistas over the gulf of Salerno from Casa Angelina's Junior Suite. Relax in style on the huge terrace, ideal for sunbathing, enjoying an evening aperitif or sharing a romantic dinner. Peace and quiet are guaranteed in the large bedroom with luxurious king-size bed.

Almost directly below Casa Angelina, La Gavitella is one of Amalfi's best beaches.

Brody House is both guest house and boutique hotel, comprising eleven unique and individually designed bedrooms for short stays. Inhabiting four buildings offering bars, recording studios, exhibition space, a private cinema and apartments for the club's members and guests, this hotel is a truly unique and exciting destination for modern honeymooners. Located in Budapest, a cultural haven that was recently touted as the "new Berlin party scene", Brody House is the ideal base for urban-loving newlyweds from which to explore this up-and-coming European city. Each room has an en-suite bathroom, some also featuring a free-standing bath in the bedroom, perfect for a decadent champagne moment to celebrate a new marriage! Every room is unique and named after a Brody House artist whose works feature in what were often their former studios. Each reveals the creative spirit of the owners and the artists, featuring vintage upcycled furniture, paint stripped walls and contemporary art.

BRODY HOUSE
BUDAPEST, HUNGARY

Architect/designer: Brody Design Team
No. of rooms: 11 rooms and suites
Recommended room: Tinei Room
Type of cuisine offered: international, seasonal
Activities: sightseeing, cultural activities, cocktail tastings

The founders named the house after Hungarian writer Sandor Brody. With a strong dedication to the emerging art scene in Budapest, the hotel's 11 rooms feature art by each room's eponymous artist.

From humble beginnings in a studio in Brody House, artist Alex Tinei is now internationally successful. Luxuriate in the room that inspired his rise to fame and absorb the rich history engrained within it.

Oía in Santorini is known for its magnificent views of the caldera. There is no better place to appreciate those views than Kirini Suites & Spa, a fairytale destination perfect for a romantic honeymoon. The luxurious resort combines elements of the Cycladic architectural tradition with luxurious living and the beautiful Aegean scenery. Pure white interiors, curved doorways and simple but elegant furnishings generate a sense of timelessness and complete tranquility in the accommodations. From the deluxe A.SPA, among the best on the island, to the unique gourmet experience, Kirini represents the epitome of high-class accommodation. Guests can relax at the outdoor swimming pool, sample a variety of Greek and international delicacies at The Pool Lounge & Cocktail Bar or savor a gourmet meal at the Anthós Restaurant. Visitors seeking rejuvenation can enjoy an ultimate pampering spa experience with a sauna, steam room, jet showers, Jacuzzi and a variety of treatments available. During sunset, guests are invited to participate in a wine tasting ceremony involving a unique selection of local produce.

KiRiNi SuiTES & SPA
OíA, SANTORiNi, GREECE

No. of rooms: 21 rooms and suites
Recommended room/villa: Honeymoon Suite
Type of cuisine offered: local Santorini products
Activities: spa, gym, swimming, excursions

This resort combines the Cycladic architectural tradition with luxurious living
and the serene scenery of the Aegean.

The impeccably chic design combined with the Mediterranean colors and the exquisite furniture creates an atmosphere of sheer romance in the Honeymoon Suite.

Situated in the lively and vibrant, cobblestoned enclave of Ortaköy, home to a famous mosque as well as a range of restaurants, cafes and clubs, the House Hotel Bosphorus resides in a building rich with history. The 19th-century Ottoman mansion at the foot of the Bosphorus Bridge is the former home of Ottoman-era architect Simon Balian, a member of the Armenian family behind many of Istanbul's landmark imperial buildings, including the Dolmabahçe and Çırağan palaces. The House Hotel's signature Turkish collaborators, Autoban, designed the hotel and combined historical glamour with contemporary design. The five-story building houses 26 rooms and suites as well as The Mansion, comprising a suite and two rooms. Featuring elegant fabrics, ornate furnishings and contemporary lighting, the accommodations represent the epitome of modern sophistication, ideal for today's newlyweds. The Bosphorus Lounge offers a stunning view stretching from the bridge to the Topkapı Palace, serving buffet breakfast, snacks and drinks.

THE HOUSE HOTEL BOSPHORUS

İSTANBUL, TURKEY

Architect (original): Simon Balian
Interior designer: Autoban
No. of rooms: 29 rooms and suites
Recommended room: Penthouse Bosphorus Suite
Type of cuisine offered: international cafe fare as well as Turkish specialties
Activities: gym, sightseeing, cultural activities, shopping, dining, clubbing

Boasting a modern Autoban chandelier, decorative moldings, a glass-walled bathroom and goose down duvet and pillows, the Penthouse Bosphorus Suite exemplifies luxurious accommodation.

The House Hotel Bosphorus is located in Ortaköy, a lively and vibrant neighborhood on the European side of the city best known for its food stalls and night life.

After a comprehensive facelift, La Mamounia has maintained its position amongst the most desired luxury addresses worldwide. The legendary palace hotel is located close to the heart of the bustling Moroccan royal city of Marrakech. It offers spectacular rooms, suites and riads, all with richly colored furnishings and ornamental fixtures. Traditional designs and patterns are integrated into every space, always combined with the most contemporary of amenities. Where Prince Al Mamoun celebrated in the 18th century, guests now dive into a modern fairy tale, replete with characterful rooms and rich with inspiration. Just a few highlights of La Mamounia are the playful décor, the stunning garden and a 2,500 square meter state-of-the-art spa. Visiting honeymooners can sate their appetites with a variety of cuisines after dipping their toes in the cultural hub of Marrakech, or indulge in a range of spa treatments.

LA MAMOUNIA
MARRAKECH, MOROCCO

Interior designer: Jacques Garcia
No. of rooms: 135 rooms, 71 suites, 3 riads
Recommended room: Executive Park Suite
Type of cuisine offered: modern interpretation of traditional Moroccan cuisine (Le Marocain), contemporary French brasserie cuisine (Le Francais), Italian treats of south Italian star cook (L'Italien)
Activities: spa, gym, swimming, cultural activities, sightseeing

Mingling Moroccan elegance with touches of contemporary refinement, Executive Park Suite offers ultimate privacy with superlative comfort. A welcome cocktail and range of local delicacies greet every guest on arrival.

Renowned as a place of glamour and haute couture, La Mamounia embodies the sensory splendors of exotic Marrakech with great discretion and grace, enduring as a beacon of Moroccan luxury and refinement.

The wildlife sanctuary Segera Retreat lies at the heart of Laikipia Plateau. Nestled between Mount Kenya to the east and the Great Rift Valley to the west, Segera is situated on 20,000 hectares of preserved land where sustainable lifestyles are focused around "4 C's": conservation, community, culture and commerce. At Segera Retreat, the unspoiled African landscape embraces guests within their own private wildlife sanctuary, an extraordinary oasis of tranquility and harmony with nature. Featuring materials such as wood, stone and thatch, the structures echo and blend with the surrounding natural landscape. Cavernous indoor spaces are adorned with an enticing combination of rustic furnishings and elaborate patterns. At the center of Segera Retreat is a large botanical garden adorned with vast numbers of plant varieties, tastefully accented by sculptures from across the continent. A diverse range of activities awaits newlyweds, from wildlife experiences and authentic and respectful cultural visits with local communities to African wine tasting and rejuvenating therapies in the wellness center.

SEGERA RETREAT
LAIKIPIA PLATEAU, KENYA

Architect/designer: LIFE Interiors + Architecture
No. of villas: 8 villas
Recommended villa: Villa Segera
Type of cuisine offered: dining at Segera is personalized and highly creative – the cook suggests a menu and location regarding the individual preferences of the guests
Activities: game drives, picnics and sundowners, guided walks, camel walks, C4C tours, sleep outs, cultural visits, helicopter trips to Mount Kenya

Segera owner Jochen Zeitz gave
G-AAMY – the yellow biplane from the
movie "Out of Africa" – a new home.

The perfect romantic retreat, Villa Segera was constructed with the utmost attention to privacy and luxury. Relax on the private veranda, take a dip in the salt-water pool, admire the villa's fine antiques and savor the spectacular views of the Laikipia Plateau.

The Retreat Selous offers an authentic and personalized game viewing experience in the middle of Africa's biggest game reserve. Blending seamlessly into its surroundings, this all-suite tented lodge nestles in wild bush by the Great Ruaha River. Three separate units on a small hill, at the river and in a private exclusive camp each offer an infinity pool as well as a variety of bars and restaurants. Interiors are luxurious but inspired by nature. Dark woods, traditional patterns and flowing fabric create an atmosphere of serenity and elegance. Guests can experience bush dining, indulge in a spa treatment and explore authentic wildlife in their own time and space – on foot, in their private open 4x4 or by boat. The Retreat is ideal for honeymooners who can spend the night in the secret Love Nest on the banks of the river or under the stars in the romantic fly camp. The retreat works in harmony with nature, wildlife and the local communities and contributes to the peaceful development of the region.

THE RETREAT SELOUS
SELOUS GAME RESERVE, TANZANIA

Architects/designers: Mohamed Ngonera, Uma Grob
No. of rooms/villas: 12 rooms and suites
Recommended room/villa: Lion River Suite
Type of cuisine offered: local and international cuisine
Activities: unforgettable game drives in Africa's biggest game reserve, boat and walking safaris, spa treatments

Featuring a personal dining area for the ultimate in romance, the Lion's River Suite is the perfect destination for a honeymoon. Experience nature first-hand with your very own safari guide before cooling off in the plunge pool and relaxing with your favorite sundowner.

The Selous Game Reserve is the largest protected wildlife sanctuary in Africa and is widely accredited as being the most pristine wilderness and one of the "secrets of Africa".

Set in a cool forest canopy of wild palms and gnarled fig trees, andBeyond Sandibe Okavango Safari Lodge looks out over spectacular delta views. The beautiful organic architecture of the lodge blends seamlessly with one of Africa's most breathtaking landscapes, making it the perfect destination for honeymooners seeking luxury and intimacy with nature. Twelve elegant and intimate suites are raised above the papyrus like the nests of golden weaver birds and feature magnificent delta views, as well as private plunge pools, cozy fireplaces and secluded nooks. Inside, the rooms become cocoons at night. Inspired by one of the Okavango Delta's most secretive inhabitants, the guest areas of andBeyond Sandibe Okavango Safari Lodge rise out of the trees clad in a wooden skin of shingles and timber that mirrors the pangolin's body armour of overlapping scales. Organic and handmade, the lodge blends perfectly with its surroundings, becoming one with the delta itself. An interactive kitchen celebrates succulent Botswana beef, artisanal breads and pizzas, while a beautifully situated massage sala offers a selection of relaxing massages in a spectacular natural setting.

ANDBEYOND SANDIBE OKAVANGO
SAFARI LODGE

OKAVANGO DELTA, BOTSWANA

Architects/designers: Michaelis Boyd & Nick Plewman Architects
No. of rooms: 12 suites
Type of cuisine offered: Pan-African cuisine
Activities: game drives, bush walks, helicopter flights

At andBeyond Sandibe Okavango Safari Lodge, the days are designed to thrill you with intimate wildlife encounters and the nights to spoil you with the romance of Africa.

Awaken in the morning to the soothing sounds of Africa as elephants splash in the water, baboons chatter and birds call in the trees. Relax in the king-size bed and look out on the delta views from beneath a dazzling white mosquito net or recline on a casual crocodile-embossed leather sofa for two.

Abu Camp offers an African experience that showcases the magnificent wildlife and landscape of the Okavango Delta. Pioneered in the early 1990s, Abu Camp offers guests an experience that will transform their perceptions of elephants, wilderness and life itself. Walk and ride with the elephants, learn about their lives and become part of the herd is a rare gift for guests of Abu Camp. Well-lit pathways link the camp's main area with the guest rooms. Using the same unique high, wide and airy canvasing style throughout the camp, the six en-suite rooms exhibit their own distinctive elegance. Blending in seamlessly with the natural surroundings, each tent is graced with generous decks and an indoor and outdoor shower. The stylish furnishings and fittings – individually chosen for each room – impart an air of opulence amid the bush setting. Allowing all guests of Abu to absorb themselves in a whole new world, the camp is a haven of peace and tranquility, immersed within the natural rhythms of the bush and perfect for honeymooners seeking an experience of a lifetime.

ABU CAMP
OKAVANGO DELTA, BOTSWANA

Architect: Paul Munnik
Interior designer: Artichoke/ Caline Williams-Wynn
No. of rooms/villas: 6 tent-style luxury units
Type of cuisine offered: international and contemporary,
African-spirited and creative cuisine of the highest standard
Activities: interaction with the Abu herd, game drives,
mokoro excursions, nature walks, Star Bed experience,
helicopter flights

A special sleeping experience is offered by the open-air Star Bed, raised above the ground. Sleep beneath the incredible canopy of stars, and let the contented rumbling and low snores of the elephants below lull you to sleep.

Abu Camp's resident elephant herd offers an unparalleled opportunity to become steeped in the African environment and transform your perception of elephants, wildlife and your outlook on life itself.

Royal Malewane is a luxury Kruger Park Safari Lodge in South Africa that exudes the romance and beauty of a bygone age whilst offering every modern-day comfort and convenience. This retreat from The Royal Portfolio is situated in the Thornybush Private Game Reserve, which boasts an astounding number of species of mammal, including the so-called 'Big Five', as well as 315 species of birds. The incredible biodiversity of the Kruger Park area makes it a special destination for nature-loving newlyweds. The surrounding landscape has a rough, wild beauty that captivates and exhilarates; the Drakensberg Mountains loom large on the horizon. A sense of timelessness pervades, allowing guests to experience the liberation of the wilderness. The lodge itself is a haven of old-world charm and stylish splendor, combining pale marble with rustic woods and textured ceilings. Large openings encourage interaction between the manmade and natural worlds. Rich tones and simple furnishings create an atmosphere of homely sophistication.

ROYAL MALEWANE
KRUGER PARK, SOUTH AFRICA

Architects/designers: Liz and Phil Biden
No. of rooms/villas: 6 suites, 2 Royal Suites (each has 2 bedrooms) and Africa House (6 bedrooms)
Recommended room/villa: Suite 3
Type of cuisine offered: international cuisine (includes a kosher kitchen)
Activities: spa, game drives, gym, swimming, helicopter flights, hot air balloon flights, canyon cruise, golf, horse riding

Life at Royal Malewane is simpler yet richer, as your senses are stirred and your heart is touched.

Boasting unparalleled views, the Royal Malewane's six palatial suites are the pinnacle of refinement and opulence in game lodge accommodation. Luxuriously appointed and fully air-conditioned, they provide an elegant colonial-style refuge in the heart of the bush.

Nestled in the foothills of the Cederberg Mountains lies an ecological oasis in a roughly hewn and magical land, offering a distinctive wilderness experience among open plains and ancient sandstone formations. This retreat is recognized for its splendid accommodation and facilities and authentic South African cuisine. With over 130 rock art sites of ancient Bushman paintings, dating from ten thousand years ago and abundant flora and fauna, this malaria and predator-free wilderness sanctuary is a magical playground, ideal for newlyweds to restore body, mind and spirit. Bush-

mans Kloof consists of 16 luxurious guest rooms and suites, as well as Koro Lodge, a private, fully-catered villa close to the main lodge. Dark woods, pale façades and stone surrounds create a sense of timelessness, while the open terraces invite indoor and outdoor spaces to merge and interact. Organic gardens provide the kitchens with fresh produce, while indigenous fynbos adds a distinctly 'Cape' dimension to a fusion of innovative and traditional fare.

BUSHMANS KLOOF WILDERNESS RESERVE & WELLNESS RETREAT
WESTERN CAPE, SOUTH AFRICA

No. of rooms: 16 rooms and suites
Recommended room: Deluxe Room
Type of cuisine offered: fusion of international and South African cuisine
Activities: spa, nature drives, guided rock art excursions, botanical walks, canoeing, archery, fly fishing, hiking, swimming

137

Exquisitely and individually designed, the Deluxe Rooms at Bushmans Kloof will invigorate the senses and quiet the mind. Cool off in one of four superb crystalline pools and unwind in your private relaxing lounge area for an indulgent and luxurious experience in this unparalleled location.

Only 270 kilometers from Cape Town, Bushmans Kloof Wilderness Reserve & Wellness retreat is the perfect place to begin your married life in a romantic setting.

Like the monumental ruins of an ancient central African civilization, Tsala's impressive stone-masonry entrance flanked by water features leads to a magnificent foyer supported by Blackwood columns. The elaborate afro-baroque décor's earthy colors, rich textures and handcrafted fittings are inspired by the diverse cultures of Africa, with the sophistication of the Western World. The views are breathtaking, whether from the exotic dining room, intimate glassed-in lounge, or large open decks high above the forest floor. Vibrant and casual with distinctive international flavors, Zinzi Restaurant offers an abundant and tasty menu, in an incredible forest setting. The African inspiration, seen in the architecture and use of natural building materials, comfortably complements the global tribal décor of beautiful, intricate carvings and metalwork from India and the fascinating patterns of the Suzani tribal textiles. Honeymooners will fall in love with the enchanting private suites, perfect for sharing intimate moments and creating lifelong memories.

TSALA TREETOP LODGE
PLETTENBERG BAY, SOUTH AFRICA

Architect: Bruce Stafford
No. of rooms/villas: 10 suites and 6 villas
Recommended room: Treetop Suite
Type of cuisine offered: international cuisine
Activities: swimming with seals, bird watching, elephant interaction, monkey sanctuary, whale watching, boat trips, sailing, surfing, kayaking

Nothing says romance quite like a crystal infinity pool, champagne on a private deck overlooking the forest, a cosy fireplace and the magic of being on honeymoon with the love of your life.

Tucked into the forest canopy, the ten luxury tree-house suites constructed of stone, wood and glass comprise a plush bedroom, an elegant sitting room with a fireplace and a spacious bathroom fit for royalty.

Located thirty kilometers from the main island of Mahé, North Island enjoys superb seclusion, pristine white beaches and a spectacular tropical interior of coconut palms and takamaka trees cradled between three granite outcrops. Purchased in 1997, the island has since been transformed by a conservation and rehabilitation program. Earlier environmental damage has been undone and a sanctuary created for indigenous Seychellois wildlife. Guests to the island's private hideaway can either explore the island alone or spend time with the environmental team, learning about the rehabilitation of this spectacular natural idyll. The island's natural beauty is reflected in the resort's architecture, featuring roughly hewn wood, neutral tones and shapes inspired by the environs. The island's beautifully decorated lounge and dining areas, scenically-located health spa and gym, and a rim-flow swimming pool are all built into a granite outcrop overlooking the azure waters of the Indian Ocean. End each day of your honeymoon at the sunset bar, tucked away on the western side of the island.

NORTH ISLAND
SEYCHELLES

Architects: Silvio Rech & Lesley Carstens
Interior designers: Maira and John Koutsoudakis (LIFE)
No. of villas: 11 villas
Recommended villa: Villa North Island
Type of cuisine offered: any menu, any venue, any time
Activities: scuba diving, snorkeling, sea kayaking, spa & gym, bike and buggy rides, fly fishing, boating and island hopping , turtle walks, dining

Perched on the granite boulders at the far end of East Beach, Villa North Island is the quintessence of privacy and seclusion. Spreading out across multi-tiered levels, it cascades down through a coconut grove to a private beach below.

Cradled in a bowl formed by three granite peaks, the luminous white beaches, lush forest, and waving palms of North Island offer a peerless and exquisite venue for the perfect honeymoon.

MAIA is located on the lush green island of Mahé on a private peninsula with a secluded beach. Situated on twelve hectares of award-winning gardens, MAIA is a pure and tranquil refuge from the cares of the world. Each of the resort's 30 villas enjoy 180 degree, uninterrupted sea views offset by the warm, earthy tones of the villa's interior design. Each villa blends perfectly with its natural surroundings, its neutral tones and natural materials paying respect to the stunning environment. Each villa comprises two separate pavilions and a private, infinity-edged pool. Newlyweds will love the resort's "whatever, whenever, wherever" concept, allowing guests to enjoy their desired meal at their preferred time and place – whether it's a late breakfast on the beach, a romantic in-villa lunch or a barbecue dinner on the helipad. MAIA's cuisine is a cornucopia of cultures, color and flavors, using only the freshest and finest ingredients and offering tastes from five different cuisines from around the world.

MAIA LUXURY RESORT & SPA
MAHÉ, SEYCHELLES

Architect/designer: Bill Bensley/Bensley Design Studios
No. of villas: 30 villas
Recommended room/villa: Villa 221 on the hilltop with a 240-degree view of the Indian Ocean
Type of cuisine offered: broad variety of dishes from the Creole, Indian, Thai, Japanese and Mediterranean cuisine
Activities: award-winning spa, snorkeling, tour of the lush gardens, kayaking, gym, diving, yoga and qi qong sessions, fishing, boat excursions, helicopter tours

When it is time to pause your frenetic pace and rediscover senses dulled by the incessant demands of life, MAIA Luxury Resort & Spa offers you a place to re-store yourselves.

Seamlessly integrated into the natural environment of the peninsula, each villa boasts a unique design and character. Revel in your own exclusive hideaway, far from the cares of the world. Take in panoramic views of the Indian Ocean or sunbathe the day away on MAIA's beautiful sandy beach.

151

This lush island sanctuary offers a unique experience in tree-house living. Newlyweds can enjoy once-in-a-lifetime views of the Indian Ocean from their sleek hilltop retreat, their every wish met by the unrivalled service of the Four Seasons staff. 67 villas and suites and 27 Four Seasons Residences descend down a lush forested incline of coconut, mango and cinnamon trees, to the private, horseshoe beach. Sophisticated but simple architecture combines with rich interior hues and luxurious furnishings. Warm woods and textured stone feature throughout the accommodations.

Standard villa features include an infinity-edge plunge pool, open-air shower, glass-walled bathroom and expansive outdoor living space with sunset views over the Indian Ocean or tropical landscape. Above the bay, the hilltop spa is home to the best natural products and epitomizes the sense of seclusion found throughout the resort. A dive center, marine education program and Tropicsurf school are also situated on site.

FOUR SEASONS RESORT SEYCHELLES
MAHÉ, SEYCHELLES

Architect/designer: Area, Bali
No. of rooms/villas: 62 villas, 5 suites, 27 Four Seasons Residences
Recommended villa: Serenity Villa
Type of cuisine offered: Creole, sushi, modern European, international
Activities: spa, water sports, marine education, surfing, diving, yoga, volleyball, coconut petanque, jogging, fitness classes

Sketch the picture-perfect setting for your very own postcard in a personalized art class by local artist Nigel Henri.

With unsurpassed views over the natural amphi-theater of Petite Anse, Serenity Villas are the perfect choice for couples. With unparalleled privacy, bask in moments of passion and tranquility in your own luxury treehouse, overlooking lush jungle, granite hillsides and dazzling turquoise waters.

Hidden from view behind an impressive carriage entrance door in oak and concealed within an old coconut grove bordering the water's edge lies one of the best kept secrets of Mauritius: the Hotel 20° Sud. The first on the island to offer the luxury and excellence of a five-star establishment within the dimensions of an attractive, privately run hotel, this is a unique and highly desirable holiday destination. It is situated in exceptional surroundings not far from the Pointe aux Canonniers at the mouth of the beautiful bay of Grand Baie. The small, intimate hotel comprises 36 bedrooms decorated with antiques as well as furniture and furnishings from the Belgian interior decorator Flamant Home interiors®. Simple, natural materials and a refined architectural style create an atmosphere of timelessness and rejuvenate the mind and senses. Newlyweds will relish the combination of refinement and exclusivity in this haven of serenity. Guests can fill their days with golf, diving or big-game fishing or relax in the hotel's spa with a hot stone massage, facial treatment or detoxifying mud wrap.

20°SUD BOUTIQUE HOTEL
GRAND BAY, MAURITIUS

Interior designer: Flamant Home interiors®
No. of rooms: 30 rooms and 6 suites
Recommended villa: Austral Suite
Type of cuisine offered: fish-based dishes, lobster menu, sushi
Activities: spa, swimming, golf, sailing, diving, fishing, excursions

The Austral Suites' private terraces are so close to the water that guests have the impression of being on a boat.

20° Sud has two more treasures in store: the oldest motorboat on the island which, when evening falls, takes a party of guests to dine under the stars on the calm waters of the bay, and the untamed wilderness of a tiny restaurant created in a ruin on Île Plate, only a catamaran ride away.

Baros Maldives is a small coral island in the Indian Ocean. Set in a translucent lagoon surrounded by a sun-drenched, golden sand beach, ringed with a colorful living coral reef, Baros Maldives is the ideal location for a romantic honeymoon. 45 thatched Beach Villas are nestled among swaying palms, while 30 Water Villas, including 15 Water Pool Villas, are poised over a shallow, shimmering lagoon. Smooth warm woods, pale fabrics and thatched roofs create an atmosphere of natural serenity. Elegant, symmetrical geometric shapes please the eye and echo the surroundings. The award-winning resort is renowned for the personal attention given to each guest. For visitors who crave complete seclusion, in-villa dining or dinner on an isolated sandbank can be arranged. Gourmet-class restaurants and an elegant cocktail lounge provide for every other desire. At the spa, newlyweds can enjoy exclusive revitalizing treatments and yoga sessions, while a luxury yacht is available to explore the dolphin-filled waters.

BAROS MALDIVES
MALE, REPUBLIC OF MALDIVES

Architect: Mohamed Shafeeq (aka Sappé)
Interior designer: Anita Indra Dewi
No. of villas: 75 villas (45 at the beach, 30 over water)
Recommended room/villa: Water Pool Villa
Type of cuisine offered: international/local, grill, fine dining
Activities: spa, diving, snorkeling, coral gardening, sandbank dining, excursions, sailing, dolphin watching, fishing

The retreat offers a coral gardening workshop which teaches guests the
method of coral propagation.

Swim in tropical seclusion in your very own swimming pool poised above the tranquil waters of a translucent lagoon. Luxuriate in the Water Pool Villa's interior decor reflecting the natural beauty of the Maldives or lounge on the timbered veranda deck and savor the glorious view.

Open from October through May, the best season for wildlife spotting, Aman-i-Khás is a wilderness camp located in a rugged brushwood forest on the fringes of Ranthambore National Park. Combining the Sanskrit word for "peace" with the Hindi word for "special", Aman-i-Khás offers accommodation in 10 luxury tents, each with soaring canopies draped in the Moghul style. Constructed of canvas and supported by a steel frame, with interior walls and ceilings draped in fine cotton, each tent has areas for sleeping, bathing and dressing. The tents are air-conditioned and can also be heated de-pending on the season and time of day. There are three separate tents for dining, spa treatments and relaxing. Perfect for nature-loving honeymooners, twice-daily, guided wildlife viewing excursions take guests into the park to spot indigenous game including tigers, leopards, hyenas, sloth bears, crocodiles and chital deer. Guests of Aman-i-Khás can also explore the region's ancient forts and colorful rural villages nearby.

AMAN-i-KHÁS
RAJASTHAN, INDIA

Architect/designer: Jean Michel Gathy
No. of rooms/villas: 10 tents
Recommended tent: Luxury Tent
Type of cuisine offered: multi cuisine
Activities: spa, safari in the Ranthambhore National Park, excursions, bird watching, nature walks, camel & horse safaris, romantic bush dinners

165

Echoes of rich Moghul traveling tents of bygone days resound through the resort's luxury accommodations. Constructed of canvas and supported by a steel frame, with interior walls and ceilings draped in fine cotton, each tent measures 108 square meters.

What could be more invigorating than waking up to the crisp morning air and walking out of your spacious tent to see the starkly beautiful wilderness of the Ranthambore National Park spread before you?

The Kandy House is a unique ancestral manor house providing seclusion and serenity for its guests in a lush, tropical garden setting close to Kandy. Built in 1804 as a decadent villa for the last Chief Minister of the Kandyan Kingdom, it has now been transformed into a designer boutique hotel. The resulting restoration sensitively blends modernized bathrooms with elegant antique furniture, while fresh touches of color complement the traditional architecture. With only nine bedrooms, the aim is to give guests an experience of staying more in a private house than a conventional hotel. In the gardens, an infinity pool has been landscaped into the hillside overlooking the rice paddy fields, the ideal spot for honeymooners to relax and unwind. More active newlyweds can enjoy exploring Sri Lanka's famous Cultural Triangle and Tea Country before returning to the hotel to savor the European fusion and Sri Lankan cuisine on offer.

THE KANDY HOUSE
AMUNUGAMA WALAUWA, SRI LANKA

Architect: Channa Daswatte
No. of rooms: 9 rooms
Recommended room/villa: Ultra Room
Type of cuisine offered: fusion cuisine with Sri Lankan ingredients
Activities: spa, excursions, swimming, bird watching, cycling, cooking classes

In 1804, the last Chief Minister of the Kandyan kingdom committed an act of "defiant decadence" – he dared to build himself a palatial villa resembling a royal residence.

Where trade winds carried legendary explorers like Marco Polo, Ibn Battuta and Fa-Hsien past Sri Lanka's soaring southern cliffs on some of history's most celebrated nautical journeys, Cape Weligama now stands as a superb honeymoon destination. Thirty minutes east of Galle, Cape Weligama inhabits 12 manicured acres atop a singular promontory rising 36 meters above the Indian Ocean. Stunning panoramas naturally complement all 39 private retreats designed by one of Asia's most celebrated architects, Lek Bunnag. Nestled strategically into the natural slopes atop Weligama's striking headland, the retreats create the welcoming illusion of a traditional Sri Lankan village. Yet beneath local terracotta-tiled rooftops, stylish interiors unfold as generously sized contemporary living quarters. An array of international dining venues captures Weligama's iconic sunsets, as does the 60-meter crescent-shaped infinity pool that appears to flow seamlessly into the shimmering sea, while those timeless breezes ensure elegant swells unfurl onto the sun-kissed sand.

CAPE WELIGAMA
WELIGAMA, SRI LANKA

Architect: Lek Bunnag
No. of rooms/villas: 39 residences and villas
Recommended villa: Ocean View Villa
Type of cuisine offered: fresh local cuisine
Activities: spa, swimming, excursions, snorkeling, kayaking, surfing, diving, sunset cruises, fishing

Postcard perfect beaches, gently breaking waves and a kaleidoscopic underwater landscape sprinkled with historic wrecks, Sri Lanka's southern coastline does not lack for magnetic charms.

Every accommodation is named after a distinguished explorer or writer such as Marco Polo or Ibn Battuta, whose historic Ceylon journey captures the spirit of Cape Weligama.

Nestled between the lush mountains and azure waters of Koh Phangan, this resort is a highly desirable destination for honeymooners. The luxurious suites and villas offer an environment of exclusive and sophisticated elegance combined with a wild tropical experience. Each suite features modern architecture infused with textures and tones traditional to Thai esthetics. Wood, bamboo and neutral colors combine to generate an impression of natural living. The interior design is highly contemporary and boasts a full range of amenities – visitors can expect the comforts of home combined with luxurious indulgences. The villas blend effortlessly into the breathtaking surroundings, inviting guests onto the white sands of Thong Nai Pan Noi Beach. Couples can also enjoy a private plunge pool, secluded amidst tropical gardens, and sate their appetites with a full menu of Thai cuisine. Breathtaking sunrises over the sea make for the ideal start to each day as a newly married couple.

ANANTARA RASANANDA VILLA RESORT & SPA KOH PHANGAN
KOH PHANGAN, THAILAND

Architect: Apiwut Sakayarojana/P49 design
No. of rooms/villas: 54 suites and 10 villas
Recommended room/villa: Ocean Pool Villa
Type of cuisine offered: fusion of international and Thai cuisine
Activities: spa, swimming, cooking classes, excursions, kayaking, gym

175

Each of the stunning Ocean Pool Villas offers a private large terrazzo tub, overlooking the calm blue sea just a few steps away.

The Anantara Rasanda has the only wine cellar with an ocean view of Koh Phangan.

Song Saa Private Island is a rare jewel in Cambodia's untouched Koh Rong Archipelago, an intimate 27-villa luxury resort spanning two pristine islands, Koh Ouen and Koh Bong. Connected by a footbridge over a marine reserve, the all-inclusive resort provides an oasis for sophisticated newlyweds seeking luxury and relaxation amid the simple beauty of its natural surroundings. Inspired by Cambodian fishing villages, the resort features over-water buildings, thatch roofs, rough-hewn natural timbers and driftwood furnishings. The resort's 27 one- and two-bedroom villas, perched overwater, on the beach or in the jungle, all provide uninterrupted views of the dramatic sunsets, seascapes and starry evenings that are commonplace for the region. Rounding out the property's offerings are a large infinity swimming pool and a yoga and meditation center. On Song Saa Private Island there is no centralised spa 'center' – the entire island is a sanctuary where regenerative sites, outdoor salas and discreet treatment villas nestle in the serenity of the rainforest and along the ocean shore. Guests looking for more adventure can enjoy sailing, diving, kayaking and snorkeling.

SONG SAA PRIVATE ISLAND
KOH OUEN, KOH RONG, CAMBODIA

Designers: Rory and Melita Hunter
No. of villas: 27 villas
Recommended villa: Overwater Villa
Type of cuisine offered: special focus on local ingredients, own organical garden
Activities: spa, yoga, underwater meditation, Song Saa nature safari, beach volleyball, treasure hunt on the island, full moon party, picknicks, star gazing, diving, snorkeling, kayaking, boat tours

Every luxury awaits in Song Saa's Overwater Villas, from huge beds dressed with Ploh linen and oversized baths to bespoke hand-crafted furniture made by local artisans.

Song Saa Private Island is as seductive as the name implies. It is Khmer for "The Sweethearts".

Alila Manggis is a secluded, stylish seaside resort in East Bali. Perfect for newlyweds, this soothing haven of serenity is set amidst a coconut grove, nestled between the sea and the majestic Mount Agung, Bali's most sacred mountain. Four two-story buildings of cool white stone, lit up in geometric beams of warm tones after dark, house the guestrooms. Each block is a skillful execution of traditional and contemporary Balinese architecture, incorporating a traditional alang alang thatched roof and a latticed screen of diagonally laid stones at each end of the lobby. Set at a 45° angle to the beach, each block is designed to allow all rooms and suites a view of the sea and the resort's palm-fringed pool. Inspired by a neighboring organic salt farm, the Seasalt Restaurant is set in a traditional Balinese pavilion on a lotus pond and serves both a contemporary menu and a range of Indonesian and Balinese favorites. Days at Alila Manggis are filled with activity and regeneration, pampering at Spa Alila, and pursuits by the sea such as discovering East Bali's legendary dive sites.

ALILA MANGGIS
BALI, INDONESIA

Architect: Kerry Hill Architects
No. of rooms: 53 rooms and two corner suites
Recommended room: Deluxe Room
Type of cuisine offered: contemporary menu and a range of Indonesian and Balinese favorites
Activities: spa, swimming, excursions

A mesmerizing and romantic back-drop for couples who want to enjoy life in East Balinese style surrounded by luxury and unspoilt nature.

Experience a taste of paradise in a Deluxe Room at Alila Manggis. Savor the glorious view across the coconut grove, the swimming pool and the sea from the private balcony. At night, relax into supreme comfort in a bed boasting down comforters and a pile of plump pillows.

The Amala is an intimate retreat located in the heart of Seminyak, Bali's most exciting and exclusive address, a heady mix of life and leisure. Its creators sought to establish the ultimate luxurious hideaway, an intimate boutique resort where couples can escape the outside world and relax and reconnect with each other thanks to the "no children below 12 years old" policy. Discreet but sophisticated, the resort's architecture invites outdoor and indoor spaces to mingle and merge with vast openings in the façades and large balconies from which to view the lush natural surroundings.

Interiors feature dark woods, warm lighting and contemporary lines. The Amala focuses on ancient Asian medicine and Western holistic philosophies and has on-site professionals who carefully assess guests' health, fitness and lifestyle to provide individualized wellness treatments. An al fresco restaurant near the main pool offers a creative cuisine that perfectly complements the resort's philosophy of achieving health through harmony. From pool to spa and restaurant to bedroom, honeymooners will find rejuvenation, serenity and wellbeing.

THE AMALA
BALI, INDONESIA

Designer: Jan Wu
No. of rooms/villas: 3 deluxe rooms, 11 villas, 1 residence
Recommended villa: Spa Villa
Type of cuisine offered: healthy cuisine with organic and raw ingredients wherever possible, adjustable to the guests's diet
Activities: spa, gym, yoga, Balinese cooking classes

187

Follow the avenue of lush green trees to the entrance of the Spa Villa, a secluded, intimate retreat. Cool off in the private plunge pool or unwind in a steam shower, scented with a selection of wild herbs.

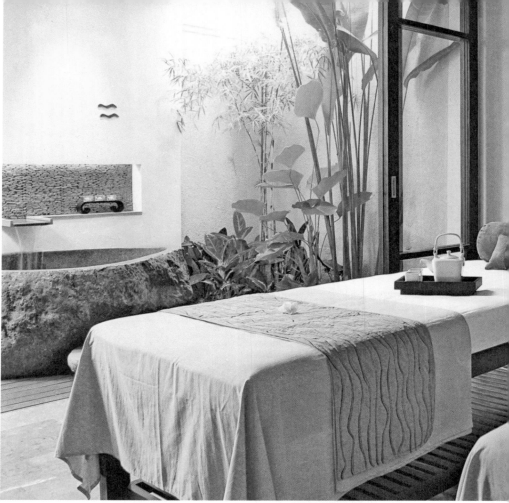

The Amala is an intimate, luxurious and blissful boutique retreat which creates the idyllic setting for lifetime memories with each other.

iNDEX

191

PiCTURE CREDiTS